a taste of
BOUNTIFUL
O·H·I·O

A Taste of
Bountiful Ohio

Favorite Recipes from Ohio's Favorite Cookbook

Susan Failor

Cover painting by Paul Patton

Illustration and decoration by Maureen O'Keefe

Foreword by James Hope

Gabriel's Horn  Publishing Co.
Bowling Green, Ohio

About the Cover, "Family Reunion on the Farm":

From the Fourth of July through Labor Day, the clans gather on farmsteads across Ohio for that cherished American ritual, the family reunion. Paul Patton, a folk artist in Maple Heights, has captured the flavor in this scene from northeast Ohio. Can't you just smell the fried chicken and hear the children playing Red Rover?

About the Frontispiece:

The state seal of Ohio portrays a land of abundance. It inspired this fanciful interpretation by Toledo artist Maureen O'Keefe.

Gabriel's Horn Publishing Co., Inc.
P.O. Box 141
Bowling Green, Ohio 43402
Editorial and business office: 419/352-1338
Orders only: 800/235-HORN (that's 4676)

00 99 98 97 96 95   10 9 8 7 6 5 4 3 2 1

ISBN 0-911861-11-4

Dedication

To all the people who have helped make the bounty of Ohio possible, including the late Janet Wood, whose love of Ohio and its food was infectious.

Contents

Foreword ix

Introduction xii

Acknowledgements xii

Chapter One

Appetizers and Beverages 3:

Boursin Cheese **4**; Black Forest Sauerkraut Balls **5**; Chalet Debonné Famous Shrimp Dip **6**; Hot Cider Punch **7**; Plain People's Lemonade **8**.

Chapter Two

Soups and Salads 9:

Beside the Point's Split Pea Soup **10**; Corn Chowder **11**; Tomato Bisque **12**; Corn and Pasta Salad **13**; Grandma Failor's Cranberry Relish **14**; Marinated Tomato Slices **15**; Waldorf Slaw Salad **16**.

Chapter Three

Breads 17:

Apple-Pumpkin Streusel Muffins **18**; Strawberry Coffeecake **19**; Zucchini-Oatmeal Bread **20**.

Chapter Four

Entrées 21:

Apple-Stuffed Pork Loin with Raspberry Sauce **22**; Bob Evans Farms Hearty Meat Loaf **23**; Cincinnati Chili **24**; George Voinovich's Favorite Pork Chops **25**; Honey-Mustard Marinated Pork Tenderloins **26**; Johnny

Marzetti **27**; Karen's Favorite Chicken Bake **28**; Smucker's Apricot Chicken **29**; Swiss Steak **30**.

Chapter Five

Vegetables 31:

Corn Pudding **32**; Fresh Country Fried Corn **33**; Fried Green Tomatoes **34**; German Potato Pancakes **35**; Potatoes Supreme **36**; Scalloped Tomato Casserole **37**; Spaghetti Squash with Garlic and Parmesan **38**.

Chapter Six

Desserts 39:

Biddie's German Apple Cake **40**; Buckeyes **41**; Di's Ohio Sour Cherry Pie **42**; Ohio Cream Sherry Pound Cake **43**; Ohio Shaker Lemon Pie **44**; Rhubarb Crunch Cake **45**; Stouffer's Original Dutch Apple Pie **46**.

Index to Recipes 47

Foreword

by James Hope

In the late fall of 1991, Susan Failor and I made a promise to each other. She would search the state for recipes that had the taste of Ohio about them. I would tour Ohio, talking to the people who make our food possible: the farmers, purveyors of food, and cooks who had stories to tell. Together, we agreed, we'd write a book with what we found.

And so we did. We spent two years at the job. Taking time from her family in Dublin and her work as food industry consultant, Sue talked to chefs, food experts, country fair judges and down-home cooks, harvesting and horse-trading recipes from Ohioans in every part of the state. She was looking for recipes that were family favorites, made good use of Ohio produce, or had an Ohio story attached to them. The best she brought home, tested in her kitchen, and—if they met her high standards for good taste, convenience and authenticity—included in our book. It was hard work, but the kind of work Sue likes: she loves cooking so much that she sometimes dreams about it.

Going my own way, I roamed the highways and byways of Ohio, having adventures outside my normal range of experience as a professor in Bowling Green. I helped harvest wine grapes, sat down to a family dinner with the Amish, talked hogs with a swine expert, drove a combine, explored the catacombs under Cleveland's historic West Side Market, and hugged Elsie the Borden Cow (who, it turns out, is alive and living right here in Ohio).

The result was a combined cookbook and travelogue named *Bountiful Ohio: Good Food and Stories from Where the Heartland Begins.* It was published late in 1993 by Gabriel's Horn Publishing Co. of Bowling Green, and it is still in print, doing nicely, thank you.

In writing our book, we came to realize what an important food producer Ohio is: one of the smaller states (34th in area) while also one of the most populated (sixth), the amazing Buckeye State has packed enough farms within mooing distance of its suburbs to be one of the nation's biggest food producers. Ohio ranks among the top 10 states in chickens, eggs, corn, oats, soybeans, milk cows, ice cream, swiss cheese, hogs and pigs, grapes, strawberries, fresh vegetables, and even mushrooms. No wonder "agribusiness"—agriculture and everything related to it—is the state's top business.

But is people who make it happen—the friendly, unassuming Midwesterners whose patchwork quilt of national origins also make Ohio one of the most diverse states in the Union. And it is to people we returned when we decided to publish reader's favorites from the more than 160 recipes in *Bountiful Ohio*.

Here—thanks to the many readers who told us the recipes they liked best of all—is *A Taste of Bountiful Ohio.*

Introduction

by Susan Failor

Ohioans love good food! This is partly because Ohio is indeed a bountiful state. From the abundant fields of corn and tomatoes to the plentiful orchards of peaches and apples, Ohioans have much to choose from.

Another reason for the love of good food in our state may be that food in Ohio is nourishment for the soul as well as the body. My favorite description of Ohio food is this: when sitting down to a good Ohio meal, you'd never ask "What is this?" You know what you are going to eat, and it looks, smells and tastes terrific. You can't wait to dig in! To many Ohio cooks, food is a sign of comfort and hospitality. Preparing a favorite recipe is a way of reaching out to say, "We're glad you're here!"

Ohioans extended that warm hospitality to James Hope and me as we travelled 33,000 miles of Ohio roads, researching *Bountiful Ohio: Good Food and Stories from Where the Heartland Begins*, the parent of the book you are holding in your hand. The more of Ohio we saw, the more we realized our book needed to be as much about Ohioans as about the food we eat. Our heartfelt thanks go to all our contributors; without them our story would not have been complete.

Acknowledgements

Many people and organizations helped with this book, but the author expresses special appreciation to that instrument of Ohio's bounty, the Ohio Department of Agriculture, Fred L. Dailey, director, and in particular to Carla Ricketts Moore, CHE, and Willis Brown, both of the Division of Markets.

a taste of
BOUNTIFUL
O·H·I·O

1
Appetizers
and Beverages

The mix of plain and fancy
in this chapter captures the diversity so typical of Ohio.
For example, homemade lemonade is a favorite refresh-
ment of the Amish, whose numbers give Ohio the largest
number of "plain people" in America. But an elegant
shrimp dip flavored by wine is just as much a part of the
flavor of the state—which is one of the nation's larger
wine producers. Travels through Amish country and visits
to the state's vineyards are among the bonuses offered
visitors to Ohio.

Boursin Cheese

Boursin cheese is a favorite fresh herb recipe of Marilyn Hartley of Hilliard. Marilyn and a friend put together an herb cookbook with some of their favorite recipes to use for teaching an herb class at Columbus' Ameriflora celebration in 1992.

Balls of boursin cheese may be made ahead of time and frozen. Marilyn often rolls them in chopped fresh parsley for a pretty variation. The mixture may be shaped into a round with a whole sprig of fresh herb pressed on top. The leftover cheese is delicious when melted over cooked vegetables.

Makes 3 cups

2 (8-ounce) packages cream cheese, softened
1 cup butter or margarine, softened
2 cloves garlic, finely chopped
1 tablespoon each chopped fresh basil, chives, marjoram, and parsley leaves OR 1 teaspoon each, dried
1 teaspoon chopped fresh thyme leaves OR 1/2 teaspoon dried
1/4 teaspoon pepper

In small mixer bowl, beat cream cheese and butter until smooth. Add remaining ingredients; mix well. Chill slightly; form into balls or logs. Wrap tightly in plastic wrap; store in refrigerator. Before serving, bring to room temperature. Serve with crackers or assorted fresh vegetables.

Black Forest Sauerkraut Balls

The Black Forest Restaurant is said to be the only authentic German-owned restaurant in the Cincinnati area. George Fraundorfer, a fifth-generation restauranteur, has created a little piece of the Bavarian Alps in the Queen City.

The Black Forest (8675 Cincinnati-Columbus Road, Westchester, 513/777-7600) serves authentic Bavarian dishes or recipes Fraundorfer has developed over the years. German bands entertain every Friday and Saturday evening. The restaurant is decorated with German memorabilia, including a stuffed Walperdinger (a must see!). On May 1 a Maypole is set up and a Bavarianfest held. A "Fest Platter" that includes sauerkraut, red cabbage, hosenfeffer, weisswurst and Oktoberfest chicken is served.

These Sauerkraut Balls took first place in the 1987 "Taste of Cincinnati" contest.

Makes 8 to 10 appetizer servings

1 pound bulk pork sausage
2 tablespoons chopped onion
1 cup (4 ounces) sauerkraut,
   drained and cut
4 ounces cream cheese
1 egg, slightly beaten
1 tablespoon flour
1 teaspoon dry mustard
Salt
Pepper
2 cups milk
3 eggs, slightly beaten
2 cups dry bread crumbs
Vegetable oil for frying

In medium skillet, cook sausage and onions until sausage is gray in color; remove from heat. Add sauerkraut, cream cheese, egg, flour, mustard, salt and pepper to taste; mix well. Roll into 1-inch balls; place in freezer until partially frozen.

In medium bowl, combine milk and eggs. Drop each ball in egg mixture, then roll in bread crumbs. In large skillet, pour oil to a depth of about 1/2-inch; fry balls in hot oil about 5 minutes or until golden brown. Remove from skillet; drain on paper towels. Serve with seafood cocktail sauce.

Chalet Debonné Famous Shrimp Dip

Beth Debevc, of Chalet Debonné calls this her "famous" shrimp dip because it is the recipe for which she gets the most requests. Chalet Debonné Vineyards in Madison (7734 Doty Road, 216/466-3485) is the largest family winery in the state and one of the most progressive wine operations in the country. The winery began producing wine in the mid-1970s from native American *Labrusca* varieties. But with an eye to the future, the Debevcs hired professional oenologist, Tony Carlucci, and began planting Chardonnay, Reisling, and Cabernet grapes. As a result, Chalet Debonné has won many awards for its wines and attracts the sophisticated wine drinker.

Makes about 2 cups

1 (8-ounce) package cream cheese, softened
1 cup salad dressing (not mayonnaise)
2 (6-1/2-ounce) cans tiny de-veined shrimp, rinsed and drained
1/4 cup chopped celery
1/4 cup sliced green onions
2 tablespoons Debonné Vineyards Seyval, Reisling or Reflections wine

In small mixer bowl, beat cream cheese until fluffy. Add salad dressing; beat well. Stir in remaining ingredients. Chill before serving. Serve with crackers or bagel chips.

Hot Cider Punch

Apple cider, the harder the better, was a popular drink on the frontier and for many years in Ohio's rural areas. Many farmers had orchards and would set up cider presses in them, which yielded a saleable product more convenient than apples. The cider could be put in barrels and transported on river boats. Even before the War of 1812, cider was being squeezed in "prodigious amounts" in Washington County, which fronts on the Ohio River. A thirsty Cincinnati was downriver.

This is a delicious hot cider beverage that tastes wonderful on a cool fall evening. It also has the added bonus of filling your home with a pleasing aroma!

Makes about 1-1/2 quarts

1 quart apple cider
2 cups cranberry juice cocktail
1 cup orange juice
1/2 cup firmly packed light brown sugar
4 whole allspice
4 whole cloves
2 cinnamon sticks

In large saucepan, combine ingredients; bring to a boil. Reduce heat; simmer uncovered 10 minutes. Remove spices. Serve hot in mugs with additional cinnamon sticks if desired.

Plain People's Lemonade

Lemonade is a favorite beverage among Amish and Mennonite families in Ohio. Nothing tastes better after hot, strenuous work than a tall, cool glass of lemonade. The Amish traditionally prepare lemonade by pressing sliced lemons to release the flavorful oils. However, this easy recipe with grated lemon rind seems to impart a similar flavor.

Once you make lemonade this way, it is hard to be satisfied with a commercial product!

Makes 2 quarts

1-1/2 cups sugar
1 tablespoon grated lemon rind
1/2 cup boiling water
1-1/2 cups freshly squeezed lemon
  juice (from about 6 large lemons)
6 cups cold water
Ice cubes

In jar with tight-fitting lid, combine sugar, rind and boiling water; shake until sugar dissolves. Add lemon juice; shake well. Chill. Before serving, add water and ice cubes.

2
Soups and Salads

In the rich soil of northwest Ohio's Black Swamp country, the tomato is king of the vegetables. Thousands of tons of the fruit that we think of as a vegetable are processed into soup, juice and sauce...much of it through what may be the largest food-processing plant in the world, Campbell's facility in Napoleon. The bright red of the tomato contrasts pleasingly with another color often seen in Ohio: green corn, in fields that stretch to the horizon. Understandably, both tomatoes and corn figure prominently in Ohio cooking.

Beside The Point's Split Pea Soup

Akron's fabulous West Point Market (1711 West Market Street, 216/864-2151), under the direction of proprietor Russ Vernon has become known as one of the most elegant and innovative food and wine stores between New York and California.

Carol Moore is director of "A Moveable Feast," the store's catering division. Thanks to her, no Akronite need resort to fast food after a late day at the office. The selection of prepared foods is enormous and a different meal could be brought home each night for weeks with no one ever suspecting you didn't make it yourself. Of course, you can also eat in West Point's restaurant or have a feast catered to your home.

This is Carol's choice of a "typically Ohio" recipe. Strictly Midwestern in origin, split pea soup is enhanced by West Point's special touches.

Makes about 2 quarts

8 cups water
1 (1-pound) bag split peas, rinsed
  and drained
1 ham bone with meat or 1 large
  ham hock
2 large onions, chopped
2 to 4 leeks, white part only,
  chopped
2 ribs celery, chopped (include some
  leaves)
1 large carrot, peeled and chopped
1 cup dry white wine
1 clove garlic, finely chopped
1/2 teaspoon marjoram leaves
1/4 teaspoon thyme leaves
Salt
Pepper

In large kettle, combine all ingredients except salt and pepper; bring to a boil. Reduce heat, cover and simmer 2- to 2-1/2 hours or until peas are soft. Remove ham bone; cool slightly. Remove meat from bone; return meat to kettle. Add salt and pepper to taste.

Corn Chowder

Pioneers coming to Ohio changed their recipes to include ingredients that were plentiful in their new home. Corn chowder is one example; it's just New England clam chowder that moved west. Corn was plentiful in early Ohio. In 1849 the state produced 59,000,000 bushels, making it the largest producer in the nation.

A lot has happened since 1849, but in 1993 Ohio was still the fourth largest grower of sweet corn in the nation—and the fifth largest of corn for grain.

Makes about 2 quarts

6 slices bacon, diced
1 cup chopped celery
3/4 cup chopped onion
3 cups diced potatoes
2 cups water
1 (17-ounce) can whole kernel corn,
  drained
1 (16 1/2-ounce) can cream-style corn
3 cups milk
1/2 teaspoon salt
Chopped fresh parsley

In large saucepan, cook bacon until crisp; remove from skillet. Cook celery and onion in drippings until tender. Add potatoes and water; bring to a boil. Reduce heat; cover and simmer 10 minutes or until potatoes are tender. Add bacon, corn, milk and salt; heat through. Sprinkle each serving with parsley.

Tomato Bisque

In earlier days, it was common practice for Ohioans to home can tomatoes, not only by themselves, but also in the form of concentrated soup base. To make tomato soup, all you had to do was heat the soup base in one pan and an equal amount of milk in another, then combine them. Most older community cookbook in Ohio contain at least one recipe for cream of tomato soup, sometimes called tomato bisque.

This version is easier, but no less delicious!

Makes about 1-1/2 quarts

2 cups chicken broth or stock
1 (14-1/2-ounce) can whole tomatoes, undrained and broken up
1/2 cup chopped celery
1/2 cup chopped onion
3 medium tomatoes, peeled, seeded and chopped
3 tablespoons butter or margarine
3 tablespoons flour
2 cups half-and-half or light coffee cream
1 tablespoon sugar

In large saucepan, combine broth, canned tomatoes, celery and onion; bring to a boil. Reduce heat; cover and simmer 20 minutes. In blender or food processer, puree mixture in small batches until all mixture is pureed. In same pan, cook fresh tomatoes in butter about 5 minutes; stir in flour. Add half-and-half; over low heat, cook and stir until thickened. Stir in broth mixture and sugar; heat through (do not boil).

Corn and Pasta Salad

Cleveland is a city of great ethnic diversity. Most Italian immigrants arrived in the early 1900s. Those who came from Sicily, a fruit-growing region, helped make the neighborhood called Big Italy the center of the city's fruit industry. In turn, Italian merchants built Cleveland into the state's center of the produce industry. They gave us our taste for oranges, bananas, garlic, olive oil and other delicacies.

Like other Americans, many Italians married members of other ethnic groups. This recipe is a marriage, too: it shows what can happen when Italian pasta meets Midwestern produce.

Makes 6 to 8 servings

2 cups rotini pasta, cooked and drained
1 (17-ounce) can whole kernel corn, drained
1/2 cup each chopped green pepper, red onion and sliced radishes
1/2 cup bottled Italian salad dressing
1/2 cup salsa or picante sauce
1/4 teaspoon salt
1/8 teaspoon pepper

In large bowl, combine pasta, corn, green pepper, onion and radishes. In small bowl, combine dressing, salsa, salt and pepper. Pour over pasta mixture; toss lightly. Refrigerate at least 2 hours to blend flavors.

Grandma Failor's Cranberry Relish

Our family serves jellied cranberry sauce with our turkey, but we ALWAYS serve Grandma Failor's Cranberry Relish with our holiday meals. Grandma's relish even survived Grandma. She passed away at age 80, between Thanksgiving and Christmas. After she had passed away, we still had some leftover cranberry relish in our refrigerator that she had made for Thanksgiving! We still enjoy the recipe, and never eat it without thinking fondly of Grandma.

Makes about 4 cups

2 (1-pound) bags fresh cranberries, washed, sorted and drained
3 to 4 medium oranges, UNPEELED, cut into quarters (center membrane removed)
1 cup pecans or walnuts
1 cup sugar (or to taste)

In food processor, finely chop cranberries in batches until all are chopped; place in large bowl. Finely chop oranges (yes, rind and all), then pecans; add to cranberries. Stir in sugar, sweetening to taste. Cover; refrigerate at least two days. Serve as an accompaniment to holiday meals.

Marinated Tomato Slices

The tomato was unknown to early Ohioans, but by the mid-1840s it had come into general use in all but the country districts. There it was still thought to be poisonous and useful only as an ornament. Fresh tomatoes still make good ornaments, but they make even better salads. This easy marinated tomato salad is perfect when having company for a summer barbecue.

Makes 6 servings

6 medium tomatoes, sliced crosswise into 1/2-inch slices
2/3 cup vegetable oil
1/4 cup white wine vinegar
1/4 cup sliced green onions
2 tablespoons chopped fresh parsley
1 teaspoon chopped fresh marjoram
  leaves, or 1/2 teaspoon dried
1 clove garlic, finely chopped
1/2 teaspoon salt
1/4 teaspoon pepper

In shallow serving dish, arrange tomatoes. In small bowl or jar with tight-fitting lid, combine remaining ingredients; shake well. Pour over tomatoes. Cover and refrigerate 2 to 3 hours, occasionally spooning dressing over tomatoes.

Waldorf Slaw Salad

The T. Marzetti Co. of Columbus advertises its slaw dressing as, "The best you ever slaw." Imaginative cooks use it in a variety of ways in the kitchen—as a dip for shrimp or vegetables, for example, or to add to potato, chicken or tuna salad. The following recipe is an interesting variation on the classic Waldorf Salad.

Makes 4 to 6 servings

6 cups coarsely shredded green
  cabbage
1 large all-purpose apple, cored and
  chopped
1/2 cup raisins
1 cup Marzetti Slaw Dressing
1/4 cup chopped walnuts

In large bowl, combine cabbage, apple and raisins; mix well. Add dressing; toss lightly until ingredients are lightly coated. Refrigerate at least 1 hour to blend flavors. Just before serving, add walnuts; mix well. If desired, garnish each serving with additional apples slices dipped in lemon juice to prevent browning.

3
Breads

Each year, more than a million acres of Ohio farmland are planted to wheat, used around the world for making bread. But other Ohio crops add interesting flavors to the breads Ohioans make for themselves: apples, pumpkins, strawberries, zucchini and oats among them. Examples of the bread-making genius of Ohio cooks can be seen at the Troy Strawberry Festival, the Obetz Zucchini Fest, Jackson County Apple Festival, the Circleville Pumpkin Show, and many other annual events. Those who go never leave hungry.

Apple-Pumpkin Streusel Muffins

This recipe is a favorite of Lorine Simmons, a Columbus native. She first sampled the muffins at a neighbor's home and subsequently asked for the recipe. Lorine likes to make them in the fall when the flavors of pumpkin and apples come to mind.

These muffins are best served warm from the oven, but they may be made ahead and reheated.

Makes 18 to 24 muffins

Batter:
2-1/2 cups flour
2 cups sugar
1 teaspoon ground cinnamon
1 teaspoon baking soda
1/2 teaspoon ground ginger
1/2 teaspoon salt
1/4 teaspoon ground nutmeg
2 eggs, slightly beaten
1 cup (8 ounces) canned pumpkin*
1/2 cup vegetable oil
2 cups peeled, cored and grated all-
    purpose apples
1/2 cup finely chopped nuts

* Since pumpkin usually comes packed in 16-ounce cans, use half the can and freeze the remainder for another batch of muffins at a later date. You'll need it, and not much later, either.

Topping:
1/4 cup sugar
2 tablespoons flour
1 tablespoon butter or margarine
1/2 teaspoon cinnamon

Preheat oven to 375 degrees. In large bowl, combine flour, sugar, cinnamon, baking soda, ginger, salt and nutmeg. In medium bowl combine eggs, pumpkin and oil; add to dry ingredients, stir until just moistened. Add apples and nuts. Fill paper-lined or greased muffin cups 3/4 full. Combine topping ingredients; sprinkle evenly over muffins. Bake 20 to 25 minutes or until golden brown. Cool 5 minutes; remove from pans.

Strawberry Coffeecake

I tasted this coffee cake while judging the "Coffee Cake, non-yeast" category at the 1992 Ohio State Fair and decided it belonged in this book. Its originator, Susie Kopf, lives in Westerville and hopes to have her own cake-decorating and specialty food business someday. She has been entering Ohio State Fair food competitions for over 10 years, and usually enters several categories. This recipe is one she put together for the competition. She has also used peaches, blueberries and raspberries for the filling. Easy and delicious!

Makes one 8-inch cake

Filling:
2 cups sliced fresh strawberries
1/4 cup sugar
1 tablespoon cornstarch

Cake:
2-1/4 cups flour
3/4 cup sugar
3/4 cup unsalted butter
1/2 teaspoon baking powder
1/2 teaspoon baking soda
3/4 cup buttermilk
1 egg, slightly beaten

Preheat oven to 350 degrees. In medium saucepan, combine filling ingredients; cook and stir until thickened. Remove from heat. In large bowl, combine flour and sugar; cut in butter until crumbly. Reserve 1/2 cup of mixture. Add baking powder and baking soda to remaining mixture. In small bowl, combine buttermilk and egg. Add to dry ingredients, stirring until just moistened. Turn 2/3 of batter into greased 8-inch square baking pan; top with strawberry filling. Drop remaining batter by tablespoonsful on top of strawberry filling: sprinkle with reserved crumb mixture. Bake for 35 to 40 minutes or until golden brown. Cool 15 minutes.

Zucchini-Oatmeal Bread

The Obetz Zucchini Festival, held annually since 1985, is observed the weekend before Labor Day. Over 30,000 people attended in 1992, and 2,000 loaves of zucchini bread and 3,000 zucchini burgers were sold. Recipes for zucchini bread abound. Although this recipe is not the one baked in Obetz, it is reminiscent of it. It is the favorite zucchini recipe of Evelyn Oldham, of Mount Victory. Although she and her husband no longer actively work their land, Evelyn has fond memories of the wonderful lunches she would make and take to her husband and sons out working in the fields.

Makes two 9x5-inch loaves

2 cups flour
1 cup oats
1/2 cup sugar
1/2 cup firmly packed light brown
 sugar
1 teaspoon baking powder
1 teaspoon baking soda
3/4 teaspoon ground cinnamon
1/2 teaspoon salt
3/4 cup vegetable oil
3 eggs
1 teaspoon vanilla extract
3 cups grated zucchini
1 cup chopped nuts

Preheat oven to 350 degrees. In large bowl, combine flour, oats, sugars, baking powder, baking soda, cinnamon and salt. In medium bowl, combine oil, eggs and vanilla; add to dry ingredients, stirring until just moistened. Add zucchini and nuts. Turn into two greased and floured 9x5-inch loaf pans. Bake 50 to 55 minutes or until wooden pick inserted near center comes out clean. Cool 5 minutes; remove from pans and cool completely. Store tightly wrapped in refrigerator.

4
Entrées

With a cluck-cluck here and an oink-oink there, the farmlands of Ohio are alive with the sounds of livestock. The state is the nation's fourth biggest grower of chickens and the ninth biggest of hogs and pigs. Hogs were the first livestock most pioneer farmers raised. Pork meant so much to the growth of Cincinnati that the city used to be nicknamed "Porkopolis." One weekend each September, however, that title belongs to Eaton, where more than 50,000 chops are served at the Preble County Pork Festival.

Apple-Stuffed Pork Loin with Raspberry Sauce

Nearly 180 years ago, stagecoach drivers pulled up at The Buxton Inn in Granville, Ohio. This recipe is a favorite at the inn, which former school teachers Ralph and Audrey Orr are busy restoring.

Makes 8 to 10 servings

1 cup chopped onion
1-1/2 cups chopped celery
1/2 cup butter or margarine
3 cups cored and chopped tart red
  apples
1/2 teaspoon ground allspice
1/4 teaspoon ground cardamom
5 cups dry bread cubes
1/2 cup raisins or chopped pecans
1 (3 to 4 pound) boneless double
  pork loin roast, split
Dash each garlic powder, pepper
  and salt

Raspberry Sauce
Makes 1-3/4 cups

2 cups fresh raspberries, or 2 cups
  frozen raspberries, thawed and
  undrained
1/2 cup apricot nectar
1/2 cup red currant jelly
2 tablespoons brandy (optional)
1 tablespoon honey or sugar
4 teaspoons cornstarch
1 tablespoon water

In large skillet, cook onion and celery in butter until tender. Add apples, allspice and cardamom; cook, uncovered, for 5 minutes, stirring occasionally. In large bowl, combine apple mixture with bread and raisins; toss gently until bread is coated.

Preheat oven to 350 degrees. Remove string from roast; open up. Spoon half of stuffing over roast; replace other half, tie with string to secure. Place remaining stuffing in baking dish. Place meat in roasting pan; sprinkle with garlic powder, pepper and salt. Roast uncovered, 60 to 70 minutes or until meat thermometer registers 160 to 170 degrees. Heat remaining stuffing during last 40 minutes of roasting.

Raspberry Sauce
In medium saucepan, combine raspberries, nectar, jelly, brandy and honey. Cook until mixture boils. Strain to remove seeds. In small bowl, combine cornstarch and water; add to raspberry mixture. Cook until clear and thickened. Serve over sliced pork and stuffing.

Bob Evans Farms Hearty Meat Loaf

Bob Evans Farms, Inc., headquartered in Columbus, operates 292 restaurants in 19 states and produces and distributes a variety of food products in 26 states. From Memorial Day through Labor Day the Bob Evans Farm in Rio Grande is a popular spot to visit. It offers riding trails, canoeing, a modern riding arena, hiking, picnic facilities, and, oh yes, a sausage shop. Sausage, of course, is a key ingredient in this homey recipe.

Makes 6 to 8 servings

1/2 cup ketchup
2 teaspoons brown sugar
1 teaspoon dry mustard
1 (1-pound) roll Bob Evans Farms Original Recipe Sausage
1 pound lean ground beef
1 cup quick cooking oats
1/2 cup chopped onion
1 egg, slightly beaten
1 teaspoon salt
1/4 teaspoon pepper

Preheat oven to 350 degrees. In small bowl, combine ketchup, sugar and mustard. In large bowl, combine remaining ingredients and 1/3 cup sauce; mix well. In 13x9-inch baking dish, shape into loaf. Bake 1 hour; remove from oven. Spoon remaining sauce over loaf; bake an additional 10 minutes.

MICROWAVE: Mix meat loaf as directed above. In 9-inch pie plate or casserole, shape into ring; cook at 100% power (high) 13 to 15 minutes or until loaf is firm, turning twice during cooking. Spoon remaining sauce over loaf; cook at 100% power 3 minutes. Let stand 5 minutes before serving.

Cincinnati Chili

Chili is as much a part of Cincinnati culture as the Reds and the Bengals; it almost seems as if there is a chili parlor on every corner. Adding cinnamon to the chili and simmering the meat in water so it is fine-textured are hallmarks of fine Cincinnati chili.

In a Cincinnati chili parlor, you must know the lingo. For basic "three-way chili," chili is ladled on spaghetti and topped with cheese. Pass the oyster crackers. For "four-way chili," add chopped onion. For "five-way chili," spoon kidney beans on top.

This is the favorite Cincinnati chili recipe of Joyce Rosencrans, food editor for the Cincinnati Post. Over the years, Joyce has become well acquainted with what Cincinnatians love to eat.

Makes 1-1/2 quarts

2 pounds lean ground beef
2 medium onions, chopped
4 cups water
1 (16-ounce) can whole tomatoes, undrained and broken up
1 tablespoon chili powder
2 bay leaves
2 teaspoons ground cumin
1-1/2 teaspoons ground allspice
1-1/2 teaspoons salt
1-1/2 teaspoons vinegar
1 teaspoon cayenne pepper
1 teaspoon ground cinnamon
1 teaspoon Worcestershire sauce
1/2 teaspoon garlic powder

Optional:
8 ounces spaghetti, cooked and drained
1-1/2 cups shredded Cheddar cheese
Oyster crackers
1 cup chopped onion
1 (16-ounce) can kidney beans, heated

In large kettle, combine ground beef, onions and water; simmer until beef browns. Add tomatoes, chili powder, bay leaves, cumin, allspice, salt, vinegar, cayenne, cinnamon, Worcestershire and garlic powder; bring to a boil. Cover; reduce heat and simmer 3 hours, stirring frequently. (If possible, make ahead of time; refrigerate, skim fat off top.)

George Voinovich's Favorite Pork Chops

This savory pork chop dish is a recipe from the *Family Favorites* cookbook written by Janet Voinovich and Fran DeWine in 1990. Mrs. Voinovich says the Governor likes these pork chops served with rice and broccoli. The aroma of the sauce is heavenly!

Makes 6 to 8 servings

6 to 8 loin pork chops
Pepper
3/4 cup apple cider or juice
1/2 cup firmly packed light brown
  sugar
1/2 cup soy sauce
3 tablespoons catsup
2 tablespoons cornstarch
1/2 teaspoon ground ginger
2 all-purpose apples, cored and
  sliced in rings

Preheat oven to 350 degrees. Arrange chops in single layer in lightly greased 13x9-inch baking dish. Season with pepper; cover with foil and bake for 30 minutes. Drain; turn chops over. In small saucepan, combine remaining ingredients except apples. Cook and stir until thickened. Top chops with apple rings; pour sauce over. Cover with foil; bake an additional 30 minutes.

Honey-Mustard Marinated Pork Tenderloins

Every August, Hamilton hosts the Ohio Honey Festival. Visitors enjoy honey in ice cream, Greek pastries, hard candy and honey butter. Entertainment includes the Little Miss Honey Bee contest. This savory marinated pork tenderloin, cooked on a barbecue grill, was inspired by what the Festival people do with honey. It is a favorite of my family.

Makes 4 to 6 servings

2 pork tenderloins (about 1-1/2
  pounds)
1/3 cup vegetable oil
1/4 cup red wine vinegar
3 tablespoons brown sugar
3 tablespoons honey
5 teaspoons Dijon-style mustard

Partially slit tenderloins lengthwise, being careful not to cut all the way through; arrange in shallow glass dish or resealable plastic bag. In small bowl, combine remaining ingredients; pour over meat. Refrigerate 6 hours or overnight Remove meat from marinade; grill or broil as desired, basting frequently with marinade. Slice crosswise, in 1/2-inch slices.

Johnny Marzetti

The story behind the T. Marzetti Company began in 1896, when 13-year old Teresa Marzetti left her home near Florence, Italy, and came to Columbus. From 1901 until 1972—the year of Teresa's death—there were Marzetti restaurants in Columbus. Today, Marzetti's is known for its salad dressings instead.

The following recipe is similar to the casserole served at Marzetti's early restaurant. Almost every Ohio community cookbook has a different recipe for this dish. It has been a favorite over the years among budget-pinched students, mothers of large families, and anyone needing an economical dish to pass at a social gathering. It also makes a good dinner for a busy family, as it can be prepared ahead of time and reheated before serving. Team it up with a salad and crusty bread, and it makes a complete, satisfying meal.

Makes 4 to 6 servings

1 to 1-1/2 pounds lean ground beef
1 cup sliced fresh mushrooms
1/2 cup each chopped celery, green
  pepper and onion
2 cloves garlic, finely chopped
1 (16-ounce) can tomatoes,
  undrained and broken up
1 (8-ounce) can tomato sauce
1/2 teaspoon salt
1/8 teaspoon pepper
1 (8-ounce) package elbow macaroni, cooked and drained
2 cups (8 ounces) shredded Cheddar
  cheese

In large skillet, brown ground beef; drain. Add mushrooms, celery, green pepper, onion, and garlic; cook 5 minutes. Add tomatoes, tomato sauce, salt and pepper; bring to a boil. Reduce heat; add macaroni and cheese. Serve immediately, or place mixture in 2-quart baking dish; refrigerate. Bake at 350 degrees for 45 to 50 minutes or until hot.

Karen's Favorite Chicken Bake

Veda Rose is the manager of product services for Borden Foodservice in Columbus. The wonder of this recipe is that it is easy to put together, yet elegant enough to impress. Veda got the recipe from her sister, Kay Anne Day, who was born and raised in Ohio, but now lives in Philadelphia. The dish is named for Kay's daughter.

Makes 4 servings

4 skinless, boneless chicken breast halves
4 slices (about 4 ounces) Swiss cheese
1 (10-3/4 ounce) can cream of mushroom soup
1/2 cup dry white wine
2 cups herb-seasoned stuffing mix
1/2 cup butter or margarine, melted

Preheat oven to 350 degrees. In 8-inch square baking dish, place chicken breasts; top with cheese slices. In medium saucepan, combine soup and wine; heat. Pour soup mixture over chicken. In medium bowl, combine stuffing mix and butter. Sprinkle evenly over soup mixture. Bake uncovered, 1 hour or until golden brown.

Smucker's Apricot Chicken

The J. M. Smucker Company of Orrville calls itself America's number-one producer of jams, jellies, preserves, ice cream toppings and fruit syrups! It began in Orrville in 1897 when John Smucker opened a cider mill and signed the paper lid on each crock of apple butter. Company headquarters are still in Orrville, on Strawberry Lane.

Vickie Limbach, communications manager, suggests serving this chicken with hot cooked rice. There is plenty of sauce from the chicken to spoon over it.

Makes 4 to 6 servings

1 (2-1/2- to 3-pound) broiler fryer chicken, cut up
1/2 cup Smucker's Apricot Preserves
1/4 cup chopped onion
2 tablespoons soy sauce
1 tablespoon lemon juice
1 tablespoon chopped fresh parsley
1/8 teaspoon oregano leaves

In shallow glass-dish, or resealable plastic bag, place chicken pieces. In small bowl or jar with tight-fitting lid, combine remaining ingredients; shake well. Pour over chicken. Cover; refrigerate 6 hours or overnight. Preheat oven to 350 degrees. Drain chicken, reserving marinade. Place chicken on 15x10-inch jelly roll pan; bake 45 to 50 minutes or until chicken is tender and lightly browned, basting occasionally with marinade.

Swiss Steak

Any Ohio community cookbook you look in is sure to have a recipe for Swiss Steak. It is a stick-to-the-ribs dish that's especially good during winter months. Many variations exist, but basically Swiss Steak is round steak cooked until tender in a tomato-vegetable gravy.

Many recipes are more complicated, but I have not found another my family likes as well. If your schedule permits, the meat can be browned and then put in your crock pot with other ingredients and cooked on low for 8 to 10 hours.

Makes 4 to 6 servings

1/4 cup flour
1/2 teaspoon salt
1/8 teaspoon pepper
1 (1-1/2- to 2-pound) round steak,
  cut into serving-size pieces
2 tablespoons vegetable oil
1 (28-ounce) can tomatoes,
  undrained and broken up
1 rib celery, chopped
1 medium onion, peeled and sliced
1 tablespoon bottled steak sauce

In shallow dish, combine flour, salt and pepper: coat both sides of steak pieces with mixture. In large skillet, brown steak in oil; remove from pan. Drain excess fat; return steak to skillet. Add remaining ingredients: bring to a boil. Reduce heat; cover and simmer 1-1/2 to 2 hours or until tender. If desired, thicken gravy with additional flour dissolved in a small amount of water.

5
Vegetables

Big farms of corn, wheat and soybeans give color and texture to much of the state—but another kind of farm is growing in Ohio. These are the small farms of people who believe in organic and sustainable agriculture, in preserving the family farm and eating from their own landscape. Many of these farmers are members of the Ohio Ecological Food and Farm Association. Big Ag still delivers most of our food, but Little Ag's influence is profound. Both are part of the flavor of Ohio.

Corn Pudding

Ohioans have various names for this dish: scalloped corn, corn custard and corn au gratin. Corn pudding is a side dish prepared with corn, cream or milk and eggs, baked into a custard-like mixture. For many in Ohio, it is a tradition at Thanksgiving, while others prepare it when fresh corn is most plentiful.

Makes 6 to 8 servings

3/4 cup milk
1 (17-ounce) can whole kernel corn, drained
1 (16-1/2-ounce) can cream style corn
1-1/4 cups crushed rich, butter-flavored crackers
2 tablespoons chopped onion
2 eggs, slightly beaten
2 teaspoons sugar
1/2 teaspoon salt
1/8 teaspoon pepper
1 tablespoon butter or margarine, melted
1/8 teaspoon ground nutmeg

Preheat oven to 350 degrees. In large saucepan, heat milk; remove from heat. Stir in corn, 1 cup crushed crackers, onion, eggs, sugar, salt and pepper. Pour into lightly greased 1 1/2 quart baking dish. In small bowl, combine remaining crushed crackers, butter and nutmeg. Sprinkle on top of corn mixture. Bake 30 to 35 minutes or until set.

Fresh Country Fried Corn

Ohioans love eating sweet corn off the cob, but fried corn is an enjoyable alternative. (It's useful, too, for those who have new dentures or who are temporarily without front teeth!) Ohio community cookbooks provide many different fried corn recipes; this one is outstanding. The cream adds a pleasant variation.

Makes 4 to 6 servings

3 cups whole kernel corn (frozen or fresh)
1/2 cup sliced green onions
1/2 teaspoon thyme leaves
1/2 teaspoon salt
1/8 teaspoon pepper
1/4 cup butter or margarine
1/2 cup whipping cream or half-and-half

In a large skillet, cook all ingredients, except cream, in butter until tender. Add cream. Cook over low heat until thickened, stirring constantly.

Fried Green Tomatoes

Fried green tomatoes have always been thought of as a down-home dish. The 1992 movie by that name caused a surge in their popularity. Fried green tomatoes are great served at brunch, but go equally well as a side dish at lunch or dinner. Or you can enjoy them at the Reynoldsburg Tomato Festival, held each September. Vendors there also offer tomato cookies, green tomato pie, tomato fudge and tomato marmalade.

Makes 4 servings

1 cup yellow cornmeal
1/2 cup flour
1/4 teaspoon salt
1/8 teaspoon pepper
6 green tomatoes, sliced crosswise
  into 1/2-inch slices
Vegetable oil
2 tablespoons brown sugar

In shallow dish, combine cornmeal, flour, salt and pepper. Coat both sides of tomatoes with mixture, pressing firmly so mixture adheres evenly. In large skillet, pour oil to a depth of about 1/4-inch; add tomatoes to hot oil without crowding. Sprinkle lightly with sugar. Fry 2 minutes on each side or until golden brown; sprinkle with sugar again after tomatoes are turned. Remove from skillet; drain on paper towels.

German Potato Pancakes

German settlers to Ohio brought many of their favorite dishes from the old country. What would we do without sauerkraut, red cabbage, or of course, German potato pancakes? They are a favorite part of any German meal. Delicious served with Sauerbraten or Wiener Schnitzel, they are hearty enough to be served as an entreé, with sour cream and applesauce, of course!

Makes 4 to 6 servings

4 medium potatoes, grated
1 medium onion, grated
2 eggs, slightly beaten
2 tablespoons flour
1/2 teaspoon baking powder
1/2 teaspoon salt
1/8 teaspoon pepper
Vegetable oil
Applesauce
Sour cream

In medium bowl, cover potatoes with cold water; let stand for 10 minutes. Drain well; return to bowl. Add onion, eggs, flour, baking powder, salt and pepper; mix well. In large skillet, pour oil to a depth of about 1/4-inch; drop 2 to 3 tablespoons of mixture from spoon into hot oil, flatten with back of spoon. Fry 3 minutes on each side or until golden brown. Remove from skillet and drain on paper towels. Serve with applesauce and/or sour cream. Serve immediately after frying, or keep warm on a baking sheet lined with paper towels at a low oven setting.

Potatoes Supreme

Scalloped potatoes—thinly sliced potatoes baked in a cream sauce—are a
favorite Amish side dish. This updated version of scalloped potatoes is a
favorite at my house. Whenever we are having a special dinner, my
husband, Bill, requests this side dish.

Makes 6 to 8 servings

*2 cups (8 ounces) shredded cheddar
  cheese*
1-1/2 cups sour cream
*1 (10 3/4-ounce) can cream of
  chicken soup*
1 cup chopped onion
1/2 cup butter or margarine, melted
1/4 teaspoon pepper
*1 (2-pound) package frozen hashed
  brown potatoes, thawed*
1 cup crushed potato chips

*Preheat oven to 350 degrees. In
large bowl, combine all ingredients
except hashed browns and potato
chips; mix well. Stir in hashed
browns. Turn into lightly greased
9x13-inch baking dish. Top with
potato chips. Bake 1 hour or until
golden brown.*

Scalloped Tomato Casserole

The Centennial Buckeye Cookbook was published by the women of the First Congregational Church, Marysville, in 1876. Editor Estelle Wilcox (1849-1943) set out to publish a book by women who were "good book-makers and good bread makers." The book sold over 6,000 copies the first year printed. In 1877, Estelle and her husband bought the copyright to the book and published a second edition, entitled *Buckeye Cookery and Practical Housekeeping*. Dedicated to "those plucky housewives who master their work instead of allowing it to master them," it became a best-seller and was re-published over 30 times. The 1880 edition contains a recipe for "Escaloped Tomatoes," so the history of this dish goes back more than 100 years. The recipe has more ingredients, but it is nice to know Ohio families have been enjoying scalloped tomatoes for such a long time.

Makes 6 servings

6 slices bacon, diced
1/2 cup chopped celery
1/2 cup chopped onion
1 (28-ounce) can tomatoes,
  undrained and broken up
4 slices firm textured bread, torn
  into pieces
1 tablespoon brown sugar
1/2 teaspoon salt
1/2 teaspoon summer savory leaves
1/4 teaspoon pepper
2 tablespoons butter or margarine
2 tablespoons grated Parmesan
  cheese

Preheat oven to 350 degrees. In large skillet, cook bacon until crisp; drain off all but 2 table-spoons drippings. Add celery and onion; cook until tender. Add remaining ingredients except butter and cheese; mix well. Turn into lightly greased 1-1/2 quart baking dish. Dot with butter and sprinkle with cheese. Bake 30 minutes or until bubbly.

Spaghetti Squash with Garlic and Parmesan

Molly and Ted Bartlett own Silver Creek Farm in Hiram, an organic farm raising fresh produce certified by the Ohio Ecological Food and Farm Association. Molly gets many requests for recipes using what they grow. Customers are always looking for new ways to prepare the many varieties of squash. This is one of her favorites. Microwave cooking makes spaghetti squash quick and easy to prepare.

Makes 6 to 8 servings

1 (2- to 3- pound) spaghetti squash
1/4 cup grated Parmesan cheese
2 tablespoons butter or margarine
2 to 3 cloves garlic, finely chopped
Salt
Pepper
Chopped fresh parsley

Pierce squash in several places with large fork or knife. Place on paper towel in microwave oven. Cook on 100% power for 10 minutes or until squash yields to pressure and feels soft. Cool slightly; halve crosswise. Scoop out seeds and fibers; twist out long strands of pulp with fork, place in 2-quart microproof baking dish. Add remaining ingredients, except parsley; mix well. Cover; cook at 100% power (high) for 4 to 6 minutes or until heated through. Top with parsley.

6
Desserts

With an Ohio dessert, you may get more than something sweet: it's apt to have a tradition with it. For example, Ohioans have a semi-official state candy: the Buckeye, a name that makes patriots' hearts beat faster. Consider the sweet wonders of the Shakers, who at one time had four communities in Ohio. The Shakers are gone now, but their lemon pie lives on. So, too, does Stouffer's Original Dutch Apple Pie, which has been delighting Ohioans for over 70 years. So eat, enjoy—and remember.

Biddie's German Apple Cake

This cake is a specialty at Biddie's Coach House in the historical village area of Dublin. The building was constructed in the mid-1800s and at one time was a stagecoach stop. "Biddie" is owner Mary Marsalka's mother and hostess at the quaint tea room. Hand-painted murals of Ohio countryside, quilt tablecloths and English china cups and saucers complement a unique menu. Culinary favorites are delicious hot or chilled soups, chicken or spinach salads, and baked brie served with sourdough bread. Please leave room for dessert, be it this luscious Apple Cake, or the signature "Flower Pot Dessert."

Makes one 13x9-inch cake

Cake:
2 cups flour
2 cups sugar
1 cup vegetable oil
3 eggs
2 teaspoons ground cinnamon
1 teaspoon vanilla extract
1 teaspoon baking soda
1/2 teaspoon salt
4 cups pared, cored and chopped all-purpose apples
1 cup chopped pecans

Frosting:
1 (8-ounce) package cream cheese, softened
1-1/2 cups confectioners' sugar
3 tablespoons butter or margarine, softened
1 teaspoon vanilla extract

Preheat oven to 350 degrees. In large bowl, combine flour, sugar, oil, eggs, cinnamon, vanilla, soda and salt; mix well. Stir in apples and pecans. Pour into greased and floured 13x9-inch baking dish. Bake 45 to 50 minutes or until wooden pick inserted near center comes out clean. Cool 20 to 30 minutes. In small mixer bowl, combine frosting ingredients; beat until light and creamy. Spread on cake.

Buckeyes

The state tree of Ohio is *Aesculus glabra* or horse chestnut, known as the buckeye. Ohioans are nicknamed Buckeyes, and so is the Ohio State University football team. And if there were an official state candy, it would be...the Buckeye.

Recipes for Buckeyes vary, but this one is the favorite of Sue Dawson. Sue is a home economist and food editor of the Columbus Dispatch. She and Dispatch food writer Karin Welzel have made the paper a major source of recipes for central Ohioans.

Makes about 3 pounds candy

1 (16-ounce) box confectioners' sugar
1 (18-ounce) jar creamy peanut butter
1/2 cup butter or margarine, softened
1 (12-ounce) package semisweet chocolate morsels
1 (1-inch) square paraffin wax

In large mixer bowl, combine sugar, peanut butter and butter; beat well. Roll mixture into 3/4-inch balls and place on waxed paper.

In top of double boiler, over hot water, melt chocolate morsels and paraffin. Stick a toothpick into each peanut butter ball; dip in warm chocolate so all but tip of ball is covered. Let excess chocolate drip back into pan. Place on waxed paper; remove toothpick. Repeat until all balls have been dipped. With fingers, pinch toothpick holes closed; smooth top. Refrigerate.

Di's Ohio Sour Cherry Pie

This recipe won Diane Cordial of Powell the Grand Prize at Crisco's American Pie Celebration National Championship in 1991. Crisco, of course, is a product of Ohio-based Procter & Gamble. Way to go, Bucks!

Makes one 9-inch pie

Filling:
1-1/4 cups sugar
1/4 cup cornstarch
1 (20-ounce) bag frozen,
  unsweetened, pitted tart cherries,
  thawed (4 cups)
2 tablespoons butter or margarine
1/2 teaspoon almond extract
1/2 teaspoon vanilla extract
1 to 2 drops red food color
Pastry for 2-crust pie
1 tablespoon milk
1 tablespoon sugar

In medium saucepan, combine 1-1/4 cups sugar and cornstarch; add cherries. Cook and stir on medium heat until mixture comes to a boil. Remove from heat; stir in butter, extracts and food color. Let stand for one hour at room temperature.

Preheat oven to 375 degrees. Divide pastry dough in half; on lightly floured surface, roll each half out to 1/8-inch thickness. Line pie plate; trim edges even with plate. Turn cherry filling into pastry lined plate. Moisten edges of pastry in pie plate; lift second pastry circle onto filling. Trim 1/2-inch beyond edge of pie plate; fold top edge under bottom crust, flute edges. Brush top of pie with milk; sprinkle with 1 tablespoon sugar. With sharp knife, slit top pastry in several spots for steam vents. Bake 35 to 40 minutes or until golden brown.

Ohio Cream Sherry Pound Cake

This unusual recipe is made with award-winning No. 44 Cream Sherry from Meier's Wine Cellars in Silverton. Meier's is Ohio's oldest and largest winery and their cream sherry is often touted as the best made in the United States. Its smooth, sweet, slightly "nutty" flavor adds a unique touch to this easy to prepare pound cake. Your guests will wonder what gives the cake such delicious flavor.

Makes one 10-inch cake

1 (18-1/4-ounce) package yellow cake mix
1 (4-serving size) package instant vanilla flavor pudding mix
3/4 cup Meier's No. 44 Premium American Cream Sherry
3/4 cup vegetable oil
4 eggs
1/2 teaspoon ground nutmeg
Confectioners' sugar

Preheat oven to 350 degrees. In large mixer bowl, combine cake mix, pudding mix, cream sherry and oil. Beat on low speed until moistened; add eggs one at a time, beat well after each addition. Add nutmeg; beat on medium-high speed 6 minutes. Pour into greased and floured 10-inch bundt pan; bake 40 to 45 minutes or until wooden pick inserted near center comes out clean. Cool 5 minutes; remove from pan. Cool. Sprinkle with confectioners' sugar.

Ohio Shaker Lemon Pie

Few people realize the prosperous suburb of Cleveland called Shaker Heights was once a thriving community known as the North Union society of Shakers. The city may be the only one in the United States named for the Shakers, but it is also a place Shakers lived for many years and none of the buildings remain. The Shakers established North Union as a settlement where they could combine their devoutly religious beliefs with an agrarian economy based on simplicity and humility.

This lemon pie recipe is a good example of Shaker frugality. Even the lemon rind is not wasted and used to impart a unique appearance and flavor.

Makes one 9-inch pie

2 lemons (rind on, ends cut off)
  sliced very thin
2 cups sugar
Pastry for 2-crust pie
4 eggs, slightly beaten

In large bowl, combine lemons and sugar; mix well. Let stand for at least 2 hours. Preheat oven to 450 degrees. Divide pastry dough in half; on lightly floured surface, roll each half out to 1/8-inch thickness. Line pie plate; trim edges even with plate. Add eggs to lemon mixture; mix well. Turn lemon mixture into pastry lined plate. Moisten edges of pastry in pie plate; lift second pastry circle onto filling. Trim 1/2-inch beyond edge of pie plate; fold top edge under bottom crust, flute edges. With sharp knife, slit top pastry in several spots for steam vents. Bake 15 minutes. Reduce oven temperature to 400 degrees; bake 10 to 15 minutes or until knife inserted near center comes out clean.

Rhubarb Crunch Cake

Lawrence Dunn was born in Sidney and lived in Piqua for 67 years before moving to Celina. Mr. Dunn, who is over 90 years old, does all the baking in his family! He became interested in baking when he married for the third time, at age 73. He also bakes black walnut cookies and angel food cakes, but says this rhubarb cake is his favorite.

This moist cake is delicious as is or can be served with a topping of whipped cream or ice cream. If fresh rhubarb is not available, frozen works well, too.

Makes one 13x9-inch cake

Cake:
2 cups rhubarb, cut into 1/2-inch
  pieces
2 tablespoons flour
1-1/2 cups sugar
1/2 cup solid vegetable shortening
1 egg
2 cups flour
1 teaspoon baking soda
1/2 teaspoon salt
1 cup buttermilk
1 teaspoon vanilla

Topping:
3/4 cup sugar
1 teaspoon ground cinnamon
1/4 cup butter or margarine, softened

Preheat oven to 350 degrees. In medium bowl, combine rhubarb and 2 tablespoons flour; toss gently until rhubarb is lightly coated. In large mixer bowl, combine sugar and shortening; beat well. Add egg; beat well. Sift together 2 cups flour, baking soda and salt; add alternately with buttermilk, stir well. Add vanilla and rhubarb. Turn into greased 13x9-inch pan.

In small bowl, combine topping ingrediants; mix until crumbly. Sprinkle evenly over cake. Bake 35 to 40 minutes or until cake springs back when touched lightly with finger.

Stouffer's Original Dutch Apple Pie

The Stouffer Food Corporation got its start in 1922 as a stand-up dairy counter run by Abraham E. Stouffer in the Arcade in downtown Cleveland. When customers began asking for dessert, his wife, Lena, would send down her own Dutch Apple Pies. Not ordinary apple pies, but ones made with fresh apples baked with cream and cinnamon sauce.

Stouffer's has probably baked and served two hundred different kinds of pies for customers over the years, but the all-time favorite has always been this Dutch Apple Pie. This is Mother Stouffer's original recipe.

Makes one 9-inch pie

Pastry:
1 cup flour
1/2 teaspoon salt
1/3 cup solid vegetable shortening or lard
2-1/2 to 3 tablespoons ice water

Filling:
4 cups peeled, cored and cubed Jonathan, Winesap or McIntosh apples
1/8 teaspoon ground cinnamon
1-3/4 cups sugar
1/4 cup flour
1/2 teaspoon salt
3 tablespoons milk
6 tablespoons light coffee cream

In medium bowl, combine flour and salt; cut in shortening until crumbly. Add water; mix lightly with a fork until dough forms a ball. Cover; chill thoroughly.

Preheat oven to 375 degrees. On lightly floured surface, roll dough to 1/8-inch thickness. Line pie plate, lifting and smoothing dough to remove air bubbles, taking care not to stretch it. Trim 1/2-inch beyond edge of pie plate; fold top edge under; flute edge. Spread apples evenly in pie shell; sprinkle with cinnamon.

In small mixer bowl, combine remaining ingredients; beat at medium speed for 8 to 10 minutes. Pour evenly over apples. Bake 1-1/4 hours or until golden brown. Serve warm.

Index

Dip, Chalet Debonné Famous Shrimp 6
Dutch Apple Pie, Stouffer's Original 46

E
Evans, Bob, Farms Hearty Meat Loaf 23

F
Fresh Country Fried Corn 33
Fried Green Tomatoes 34

G
Garlic and Parmesan, Spaghetti Squash with 38
George Voinovich's Favorite Pork Chops 25
German Apple Cake, Biddie's 40
German Potato Pancakes 35
Grandma Failor's Cranberry Relish 14
Green Tomatoes, Fried 34

H
Honey-Mustard Marinated Pork Tenderloins 26
Hot Cider Punch 7

J
Johnny Marzetti 27

K
Karen's Favorite Chicken Bake 28

L
Lemon Pie, Ohio Shaker 44
Lemonade, Plain People's 8

M
Marinated Pork Tenderloins, Honey-Mustard 26
Marinated Tomato Slices 15
Marzetti, Johnny 27
Meat Loaf, Bob Evans Farms Hearty 23
Muffins, Apple-Pumpkin Streusel 18
Mustard, Honey-, Marinated Pork Tenderloins 26

O
Oatmeal, Zucchini-, Bread 20
Ohio Cream Sherry Pound Cake 43
Ohio Sour Cherry Pie, Di's 42
Ohio Shaker Lemon Pie 44

P
Pancakes, German Potato 35
Parmesan and Garlic, Spaghetti Squash with 38
Pasta, and Corn, Salad 13
Pea Soup, Beside the Point's Split 10

A
Apple Pie, Stouffer's Original Dutch 46
Apple Cake, Biddie's German 40
Apple-Pumpkin Streusel Muffins 18
Apple-Stuffed Pork Loin with Raspberry Sauce 22
Apricot Chicken, Smucker's 29

B
Beside the Point's Split Pea Soup 10
Biddie's German Apple Cake 40
Bisque, Tomato 12
Black Forest Sauerkraut Balls 5
Bob Evans Farms Hearty Meat Loaf 23
Boursin Cheese 4
Bread, Zucchini-Oatmeal 20
Buckeyes 41

C
Cake, Biddie's German Apple 40
Cake, Ohio Cream Sherry Pound 43
Cake, Rhubarb Crunch 45
Casserole, Scalloped Tomato 37
Chalet Debonné Famous Shrimp Dip 6
Cheese, Boursin 4
Cherry Pie, Di's Ohio Sour 42
Chicken Bake, Karen's Favorite 28
Chicken, Smucker's Apricot 29
Chili, Cincinnati 24
Chowder, Corn 11
Cider Punch, Hot 7
Cincinnati Chili 24
Coffeecake, Strawberry 19
Corn Chowder 11
Corn, Fresh Country Fried 33
Corn Pudding 32
Corn and Pasta Salad 13
Country Fried Corn, Fresh 33
Cranberry Relish, Grandma Failor's 14
Cream Sherry Pound Cake, Ohio 43
Crunch Cake, Rhubarb 45

D
Di's Ohio Sour Cherry Pie 42

Pie, Ohio Shaker Lemon 44
Pie, Di's Ohio Sour Cherry 42
Pie, Stouffer's Original Dutch Apple 46
Plain People's Lemonade 8
Pork Chops, George Voinovich's Favorite 25
Pork Tenderloins, Honey-Mustard Marinated 26
Pork Loin, Apple-Stuffed, with Raspberry Sauce
    22
Potato Pancakes, German 35
Potatoes Supreme 36
Pound Cake, Ohio Cream Sherry 43
Pudding, Corn 32
Pumpkin, Apple-, Streusel Muffins 18
Punch, Hot Cider 7

R
Raspberry Sauce, with Apple-Stuffed Pork Loin
    22
Relish, Grandma Failor's Cranberry 14
Rhubarb Crunch Cake 45

S
Salad, Waldorf Slaw 16
Salad, Corn and Pasta 13
Sauce, Raspberry, with Apple-Stuffed Pork Loin
    22
Sauerkraut Balls, Black Forest 5
Scalloped Tomato Casserole 37
Shaker Lemon Pie, Ohio 44
Sherry Pound Cake, Ohio Cream 43
Shrimp Dip, Chalet Debonné Famous 6
Slaw Salad, Waldorf 16
Smucker's Apricot Chicken 29
Split Pea Soup, Beside the Point's 10
Squash, Spaghetti, with Garlic and Parmesan 38
Steak, Swiss 30
Stouffer's Original Dutch Apple Pie 46
Strawberry Coffeecake 19
Stuffed Pork Loin, Apple-, with Raspberry Sauce
    22
Swiss Steak 30

T
Tomato Slices, Marinated 15
Tomato Bisque 12
Tomato Casserole, Scalloped 37
Tomatoes, Fried Green 34

V
Voinovich's, George, Favorite Pork Chops 25

W
Waldorf Slaw Salad 16

Z
Zucchini-Oatmeal Bread 20

Ohio's favorite cookbook:

BOUNTIFUL OHIO, by James Hope and Susan Failor, published in 1993 to rave reviews, is a celebration of the food and people of the state where America's Heartland begins. This 224-page book offers 163 down-home recipes, including family treasures, chef's favorites, and country fair prize-winners. They are the wholesome flavors of good food from Heartland, tested and written by a professional home economist.

But *Bountiful Ohio* is more than a cookbook. It is filled with fascinating lore and new stories about the abundance of the state and the people who make it possible: modern-day Johnny Appleseeds, an Amish homemaker, the Angel of the Black Swamp, Mr. Pork, and many others. Anyone who loves the Heartland will enjoy this book, whether they cook from it or not.

Bountiful Ohio is handsomely designed and generously illustrated with pictures old and new. It makes an excellent gift. *Softcover:* $14.95; *hardcover:* $21.95; *signed and numbered edition limited to 100 copies:* $39.95.

Other Books of Interest from Gabriel's Horn

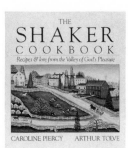

THE SHAKER COOKBOOK, Caroline Piercy and Arthur Tolve (1984). The latest revision of a classic, this 192-page book is filled with delicious, authentic recipes updated for modern convenience. And there's abundant lore and many sketches from the Shaker settlement where the Cleveland suburb of Shaker Heights is today. *Softcover:* $12.95.

"Hardy, simple, quaint recipes abound."—*Booklist.* "The cookbook is beautifully illustrated...bits of Shaker lore and verse are sprinkled throughout."—*Country Living.*

RIPSNORTING WHOPPERS!, by Rick Sowash with illustrations by Maureen O'Keefe (1994). Sowash, known throughout the Heartland as The Master of the Tall Tale, spins yarns that amused our forefathers—and are captivating modern audiences, young and old. This delightfully illustrated book has been called "a treasury of witty, wise and wonderful Americana, masterfully told." *Softcover:* $11.95; *hardcover:* $19.95. Favorites from the book are recounted by Sowash himself on 60-minute cassettes: *audio:* $9.95 and *video:* $24.95.

To order, call Gabriel's Horn Publishing Co. at

1-800-235-4676

or use order blank at the end of this book.

**To order books,
use order form
on other side.**

Order Form for Books

This form may be copied

If the book you want isn't available at your favorite store, you may order directly from the publisher. Telephone toll free 1-800-235-4676 or mail form and payment to:

Gabriel's Horn Publishing Co.
Department TBO
P.O. Box 141
Bowling Green, OH 43402

Quantity	Title and Edition	Price each	Total
_____	A TASTE OF BOUNTIFUL OHIO	$6.95	$ _____
_____	BOUNTIFUL OHIO (soft)	$14.95	$ _____
_____	BOUNTIFUL OHIO (hard)	$21.95	$ _____
_____	BOUNTIFUL OHIO (limited)	$39.95	$ _____
_____	THE SHAKER COOKBOOK (soft)	$12.95	$ _____
_____	RIPSNORTING WHOPPERS! (soft)	$11.95	$ _____
_____	RIPSNORTING WHOPPERS! (hard)	$19.95	$ _____
_____	RIPSNORTING WHOPPERS! (audio)	$9.95	$ _____
_____	RIPSNORTING WHOPPERS! (video)	$24.95	$ _____

UPS SHIPPING TO EACH ADDRESS:
$3 first item, 50¢ each thereafter. $ _____

Ohio residents add 6% tax. $ _____

TOTAL AMOUNT OF ORDER $ _____
Check or MasterCard/VISA acceptable.

Name _____

Street address _____

City _____ State _____ ZIP _____

Card no. _____ Expires _____